CULTURALLY RESPONSIVE
TEACHING AND SUPERVISION

A Handbook for
Staff Development

CULTURALLY RESPONSIVE TEACHING AND SUPERVISION

A Handbook for Staff Development

C. A. BOWERS
AND
DAVID J. FLINDERS

Teachers College, Columbia University
New York and London

Published by Teachers College Press, 1234 Amsterdam Avenue, New York, NY 10027

Library of Congress Cataloging-in-Publication Data
  Bowers, C. A.
    Culturally responsive teaching and supervision : a handbook for staff
  development / C. A. Bowers and David J. Flinders
      p. cm.
    ISBN 0-8077-3078-5 (pbk. ; alk. paper)
    1. School supervision. 2. Teacher-student relationships. 3. Classroom
  environment. I. Flinders, David J., 1955— . II. Title.
    LB2806.4.B68   1991
    371.1'024—dc20   90-25463

ISBN 0-8077-3078-5 (pbk. ; alk. paper)

Printed in the United States of America
98 97 96 95 94 93 92 91   1 2 3 4 5 6 7 8

Contents

Preface	**vii**
PART I: INTRODUCTION	**1**
Chapter 1 Conceptual Foundations	**3**
Chapter 2 What To Look For: Cultural Patterns in Perspective	**9**
Primary Socialization	10
Complexity of Language	*10*
Making Taken-for-Granted Beliefs Explicit	*11*
Historical and Cross-Cultural Perspectives	*11*
Metaphorical Basis of Thought	12
Analogic Thinking	*13*
Iconic Metaphors	*13*
Root Metaphors	*14*
Culturally Stereotyped Patterns of Thought and Values	15
Patterns of Thought Related to an Ecological Awareness	16
Nonverbal Communication	16
Orchestration of Student Involvement	18
The Role of Framing in Communication	*18*
Turn-Taking and Negotiation	*19*
Power and Solidarity in the Classroom	*20*
Gender Bias	21
Culturally Appropriate Participation Patterns	21
Chapter 3 How to Use This Handbook	**23**
Pre-observation Conferencing	24
Classroom Observations	25
Review	26
Providing Feedback	27

PART II: GUIDES FOR SUPERVISORS 29

Guide #1   **Structure of the Lesson** 30

Guide #2   **Primary Socialization** 32

Guide #3   **The Metaphorical Basis of Thought** 34

Guide #4   **Culturally Stereotyped Patterns of Thought and Values** 36

Guide #5   **Patterns of Thought Related to an Ecological Awareness** 38

Guide #6   **Mathematics Lesson** 40

Guide #7   **Science Lesson** 42

Guide #8   **Nonverbal Patterns of Communication** 44

Guide #9   **Orchestration of Student Involvement** 46

Guide #10   **Gender as a Dimension of Classroom Relationships** 48

Guide #11   **Culturally Appropriate Participation Patterns** 50

About the Authors 53

Preface

This handbook on culturally responsive supervision was written, in part, in response to fundamental changes occurring in society. The old industrial model, which has been a dominant influence on our approach to public education in recent decades, is now being viewed as both economically outmoded and based on wrong assumptions about how people best work together. There is a growing awareness on the part of different cultural groups that their traditions are essential to maintaining a sense of community and personal identity. The right of one cultural group to dominate others by setting the standards for how to think about individualism, success, technology, and so forth is also being challenged along gender lines. The deteriorating condition of the environment is further creating fault lines in the bedrock of our belief system, with some centuries-old beliefs remaining unaffected while others are being radically reformulated.

This book was also written in response to changes taking place in our most basic areas of understanding. Developments in the sciences have overturned long-held views about the role of the observer and the fixed and measurable nature of what previously was thought to be the basic structure of matter. Fundamental changes in the other areas of inquiry have been equally important in overturning long-held views about the nature of the rational process, language, and even the way cultural differences are interpreted. That language is metaphorical and encodes the experiences and thought patterns of a cultural group is just one of the insights that dislodges a keystone holding together the structure of belief that still underlies most current approaches to teacher education and classroom practices.

Although the emphasis in this handbook is on the practical (that is, what teachers and, by extension, supervisors, should be attending to in the classroom), it brings into focus aspects of the classroom that have, in the past, not been viewed as a concern either of the teacher or supervisor. These new areas of awareness—how the teacher uses metaphorical thinking to introduce a new idea, the teacher's gatekeeper role in the process of primary socialization, the problem of recognizing that behavior is a way of communicating about relationships and that behavior patterns may be influenced by the student's primary culture, how the teacher balances the exercise of power with the achievement of solidarity with the students, and so forth—reflect our attempt to bring the approach to teaching into line with recent developments in the social and natural sciences. Thinking of the classroom as an ecology of language and cultural patterns also makes more sense in terms of recent social developments.

The guides that are intended to help the supervisor keep in mind the multiple dimensions of a classroom ecology include aspects of teacher decision making that have always been part of the classroom, but generally have not been recognized because of old and now outmoded patterns of thinking. For example, attending to whether the teacher gives equal authority to the spoken and written word (in the past, the written word and literate peoples have been given a privileged status), and to whether the teacher places language in historical context, are critically important aspects of a culturally responsive approach to supervision. As both of these examples illustrate, that approach must be informed by recent developments in other fields of knowledge; it is important to recognize that old assumptions about language, individualism, behavior, and the rational process cannot be used as the basis for implementing the guides. To do so is to fall victim to the age-old problem of putting new wine into old containers.

The handbook contains brief explanations of each aspect of the classroom ecology covered by the supervision guides, but it should be recognized that these explanations, along with accompanying examples, are really not adequate in themselves, and that they should be supplemented by further readings. The theoretical foundations for each aspect of the classroom covered by the supervision guides are given chapter-length treatment in *Responsive Teaching: An Ecological Approach to Classroom Patterns of Language, Culture, and Thought* (Teachers College Press, 1990); the book also contains a bibliography for further reading.

This handbook should be viewed as a starting point upon which others may build. Our own efforts were dependent upon the help of others, and we wish to give special acknowledgement to Maggie McBride for suggestions about how a culturally responsive approach to supervision relates to teaching mathematics. We also want to thank Ray Hull for his assistance in developing the guide for a science lesson. Lastly, we wish to thank Sevilla Ludwig for the many skills she brought to typing the manuscript.

CULTURALLY RESPONSIVE TEACHING AND SUPERVISION

A Handbook for Staff Development

Part I

Introduction

CHAPTER 1

Conceptual Foundations

Observing human performance is central to the act of supervision. In business and industry, supervision is understood as part of the evaluation and management of a person's work performance. Although we use the same metaphor of "super-vision" to describe the observation of teaching, the unique contexts of classroom learning require that we realign supervision with an entirely different set of meanings and purposes. In particular, our attention is turned from the task-orientation of technical approaches to the social and cultural dimensions of school experience. Our purpose, in this brief introduction, is to explain how these contextual dimensions lead to a different way of understanding the process of supervision, one that we call "culturally responsive supervision." A second purpose is to identify what the supervisor needs to know in order to recognize and illuminate how certain patterns of teaching foster learning while other patterns tend to obstruct it. Finally, the use of the observation guides in the second half of the handbook, which we intend to serve as memory aids for the supervisor, will also be explained.

The act of observing teachers (or student teachers) and providing them with feedback about their interactions with students cannot be separated from the larger questions surrounding the purposes of education. Over the last several decades we have witnessed approaches to education that are based on widely divergent social priorities, ranging from preparing students to utilize freedoms in a self-directing manner to preparing students for the adult world of work. These examples, which reflect two extremes, suggest how pedagogical and curricular priorities have been influenced by, and are deeply rooted in, the socio-political shifts occurring in the society at large. Judging teacher effectiveness, for instance, in terms of student on-task behavior (which can be measured) would have been inappropriate in the open classrooms of the late 1960s. Similarly, the issue of whether the teacher's turn-taking patterns, humor, or use of praise reflect a gender bias is an outgrowth of more current social developments. In short, what the supervisor observes and responds to cannot be adequately understood if supervision is framed in a language that isolates the classroom from its surrounding social-political world. Thinking of supervision in terms of increasing the teacher's productivity or of helping to reduce the gap between an actual performance and an ideal performance—to cite two often held views—ignores two critically important concerns: (1) how the embeddedness of the classroom influences the priorities that guide the supervisor's act of observation, and (2) the nature of the professional relationship between supervisor and teacher.

If we consider the context of the classroom in its broadest sense, then issues relating to school dropout rates—drugs, poverty, lack of adult role models—as well as changes in the work force become important factors that impinge upon the classroom (but not always with equal force). There are also social issues relating to gender equality, a growing awareness that cultural identities should be nourished as a source of political strength and moral authority, and increasing attention given to disruptions and health threats caused by the impact of our technologies and cultural practices on the environment. The list of social concerns that reach into the classroom to affect student learning, the connections and questions that teachers might raise during a class discussion, the student's sense of whether the lesson has any relevance to the world that they understand, and so on, suggest that educational processes cannot be separated from the political pressures that seem now to encompass nearly every facet of social life. This also applies to the relationship between the supervisor and the educational processes that are being observed and evaluated. Supervision, like classroom teaching, is embedded within a cultural milieu.

This connection between supervision and the relevancy of what happens in the classroom to the political priorities of the larger society is a subtle yet vitally important one to grasp. To suggest that the supervisor can guide and evaluate a teacher's performance solely on the basis of objective data is both naive and irresponsible. On the other hand, to argue that the supervisor must evaluate teacher and student interactions strictly in terms of political priorities (even "progressive ones") is equally wrong. Although what the supervisor observes and values as good teaching cannot be separated from an ideological orientation, we want to suggest that the supervisor's role should not become partisan—particularly when many of the political issues have not been resolved in the larger society. Rather, we want to stress that the unresolved political issues related to problems of drug abuse, gender inequality, ecological disruptions, and the domination of minority groups, to cite just a few of our current social problems, should serve to *sensitize* and *inform* the supervisor's awareness of what happens in the classroom.

Although the supervisor's own beliefs (which can also be understood as ideological) introduce into the supervisor-teacher relationship a political dimension, we want to argue that it is possible to avoid the dangers surrounding both open partisanship and, to cite the other extreme, the illusion of political neutrality. The middle road we are advocating is grounded on the recognition that education is not a matter of giving students ready-made answers, as such answers are often formulated in response to an earlier and quite different set of social circumstances. Rather, education should provide students with a basis both for understanding the forms of knowledge handed down from the past and for assessing their current value and usefulness. This is essentially a process of learning to understand the continuities that connect patterns of social life: patterns from the past and the forces that shaped them; current patterns that contribute to personal and social well-being (or have detrimental consequences); and patterns that will be needed in the future, if we are to survive in ecological balance. This view of education is further grounded on a recognition that an understanding of language and culture will help to illuminate different though interrelated aspects of teaching and learning. Sensitivity to shifts in public consensus around such critical issues as work, gender, and cultural democracy (as well as an awareness of social issues that are not fully articulated or even acknowledged) must inform the supervisor's work. But it is the ability to recognize the classroom as a language/culture medium that most clearly shapes and defines the appropriate role of the supervisor.

To put this another way, the responsibilities of the supervisor are defined, in part, by the pervasive influence of language and culture on classroom activities. This influence, as we argue in *Responsive Teaching*, is often overlooked in the professional education of teachers; it has also been largely ignored in the literature dealing with the practice of supervision. Its distinctive feature has to do with the way in which language and culture (in all their interrelated and multiple dimensions) are learned largely at a taken-for-granted level. This means that we are not usually aware of culture or how language both constrains and facilitates ways of understanding. Contrary to the currently held beliefs, many critically important dimensions of knowledge are taken for granted—what can also be understood as tacit knowledge or as the cultural basis of our natural attitude. For example, thinking of time as linear, that change is progressive, that good things are associated with the spatial direction of "up" ("She is highly respected") while bad things are "down" ("He was feeling low"), and that rationality is culture-free, represent taken-for-granted knowledge that is culturally specific. Other examples—regarding how we use our bodies to send messages about how we feel toward others (nonverbal communication), and what foods taste good (even what is seen as food), and what sounds pleasant—could also be cited to illustrate the complexity and broad range of culturally based experience.

But the aspect of language and culture we want to stress as important for understanding the challenge of responsive supervision, to reiterate, is the manner in which these forms of knowledge are often hidden from the person who possesses them. Such forms of knowledge are often shared with others, including students, at an implicit level; and the way they both facilitate and bind human thought and behavior is also mostly hidden. Simply put, the depth of cultural embeddedness—even for those people who think they are autonomous and rational—cannot be made fully explicit. All of us are embedded in cultural patterns that we simply take for granted, such as when we write from left to right on a piece of paper and re-enact the thought patterns dictated by grammatical characteristics and presuppositions encoded in language.

Teachers, students, and supervisors—not to mention parents, interested citizens, and various types of educational professionals—also face this problem of thinking and acting without knowing how much of their experience is influenced by a natural attitude that is linguistically and culturally based. Data collectors will not be able to provide answers to the question of "how much?"—but that is not really the critical issue here. Rather, the central issue raised by the tacit or implicit nature of our linguistic and cultural embeddedness has to do with recognizing, in a classroom setting, when implicit patterns of understanding impede communication and have a detrimental influence on the process of learning. As this sounds far simpler than it really is, we want to cite just a few of the examples that can arise in classrooms that are increasingly composed of students and a teacher who may be members of different primary cultures.

Giving explicit attention to patterns of language and culture is useful for understanding that teachers and students do not simply use language as a conduit for sending information back and forth, and that thinking is not simply the inputting of information (even when structured by teaching to an objective). Language (and more broadly, communication) is more than just the content of spoken messages; it includes changes in voice pitch, rhythm, and the use of the body and social space as additional sources of information. The following examples suggest the range of language and cultural patterns that characterize an increasing number of classrooms today: telling stories in a linear, three-part, topic-centered manner (while some members of the class may be accustomed to an episodic pattern of story telling); using behavior patterns to establish the right to speaking turns (differences in pauses, eye contact, body gestures); fostering competition, individual achievement, and one-to-one communication (which may conflict with the more group-oriented patterns of some students); introducing new concepts through the use of metaphors that are either gender, age group, or culture specific; representing objective data and facts as the basis of thought (with some students having a natural inclination toward the authority of other forms of knowledge); and privileging literate forms of discourse (with some students being embedded in various traditions of oral discourse). Many other patterns that represent differences in language and culture could be cited. Our concern is not to compile a complete list, but to stress that students and the teacher, as members of different cultural traditions, communicate and learn from each other in an environment that might best be understood as an ecology of language and cultural patterns.

Some of the examples we cited in the previous paragraph were deliberately chosen in order to bring out how fundamental differences in the patterns might contribute to breakdowns in communication and misunderstandings of what is being taught. When students take certain patterns for granted and the teacher's natural attitude is grounded in a different set (perhaps shared only by those students from a similar cultural and class background), effective communication with all the students will be limited—and thus, the opportunities for learning will also suffer. The relationship of cultural patterns to learning, which must be orchestrated by teachers who—like the rest of us—may not be able to recognize and understand patterns that do not fit their own taken-for-granted patterns, points to a key responsibility of the supervisor. It also helps to establish the nature of a professional relationship between the supervisor and teacher that does not carry the connotations of the industrial model, in which the supervisor would stand in a hierarchical relationship above the teacher.

Culturally responsive supervision provides teachers with a third-party vantage point that may help them recognize how language and cultural patterns that they take for granted (and thus are not aware of) influence the learning environment of the classroom. The other responsibility of the supervisor is to help the teacher clarify and adapt professional judgments in a way that takes cultural differences into account. These two responsibilities will encompass many of the supervisor's traditional concerns—how the teacher asks questions and gives praise, how the teacher responds to students who are "off task," how the purposes of the lesson are initially framed and how adequately they are summarized, how much "wait time" the teacher allows before asking another question or providing the answer to students, and so forth—but these traditional concerns will be placed within a broad context of understanding.

When the teacher's behavior and thought processes are understood as cultural, and are viewed as one aspect of an ecology of culturally diverse patterns (reflecting differences of ethnicity, gender, and age group that characterize the composition of the class), these more traditional supervisory concerns will be understood in an entirely different manner. The "off task" behavior, as viewed from the Anglo, middle-class teacher's perspective, may not reflect the social interaction patterns of the student's primary culture. To cite another example, a student's silence could mean that the student simply does not know the answer to the teacher's question—or it may reflect a cultural pattern that prescribes how children should relate to adults. The ecology of language and cultural patterns that characterize the classroom thus has to be taken into account as part of the supervisor's interpretation of effective teaching.

The old view of supervision, which included collecting supposedly "objective data," was based on a view of the teacher and students as autonomous individuals, of the learning process as individually centered and dependent upon the inputting of information, and of language as a neutral conduit through which teachers and students "transmitted" their thoughts to one another. These assumptions, which have their roots in the Cartesian thinking of the 17th century, are now being recognized as culturally specific and thus limited as a basis for understanding how a student's experiences are culturally influenced.

Supervisors who viewed the classroom through the cultural lenses of a Cartesian-oriented set of assumptions also viewed themselves as autonomous individuals who could adopt an independent and neutral ("objective") stance toward what they observed. The complex interplay of culture, language, and thought within which the supervisor is embedded was simply not considered important. Culturally responsive supervision requires a fundamentally different way of viewing not only students and teachers, but also supervisors. Helping teachers recognize their own taken-for-granted patterns, and how those patterns differ from the ones that are part of the student's natural attitude, requires that supervisors become more sensitive to their own cultural embeddedness. Stated simply, there is no culture-free person, and thus there is no objective observation—except as a convention of belief. What supervisors see, and how they frame and interpret it, depends upon the assumptions and patterns they have learned and sustained as members of a cultural group. Here the implications become quite obvious: supervisors must begin to recognize their own cultural assumptions and patterns as they attempt to understand the various ways in which classroom interaction and learning are influenced by culture.

Understanding the interplay between pattern and individualized expression in those we observe (as well as in ourselves) is a long and difficult task. But recognizing that language and cultural patterns are a foundational part of human experience—including what occurs in the classroom—is a first step. We think that this starting point also provides a basis for identifying aspects of the classroom environment that previously have not been a concern of the supervisor. In order to make sense of new elements that are introduced in our supervision guides (pages 29–51), as well as reframe more traditional concerns, we will use the next section to provide a brief explanation of the educationally related processes highlighted by this approach.

CHAPTER 2

What To Look For:
Cultural Patterns in Perspective

Learning about cultural patterns of communication and thought should be viewed as an ongoing dimension of career development. Although the ideal situation would be a close alignment between professional studies and the more culturally and linguistically oriented approaches to social inquiry, this supervision guide can serve as an initial starting point. Many of the patterns identified in the guides have not traditionally been part of the knowledge base acquired by supervisors; consequently, we think that a preliminary explanation of how to recognize patterns and what significance they hold for the learning process would be useful. We wish to emphasize, however, that the explanations touch on the most basic aspects of learning and that further study will help deepen the supervisor's understanding and responsiveness to the cultural ecology of the classroom.

Our discussion is organized around the division between patterns that relate most directly to thought processes and those that have more to do with communication about relationships. These two overlapping categories include the "mental ecology" and the "social ecology" of the classroom. We also have developed three guides—"structure of the lesson," "ecology of a science lesson," and "ecology of a mathematics lesson"—that incorporate patterns deserving special treatment. The guides for lessons in science and mathematics (Guides #6 and #7) were created because these particular subject areas are often viewed as content oriented and therefore supposedly free of the cultural and linguistic patterns that are readily acknowledged as integral to the teaching of other subjects. The "structure of the lesson" (Guide #1) provides a more gestalt view of teaching and thus deserves separate consideration. The remaining guides focus on:

- Primary socialization (Guide #2)
- Metaphor (Guide #3)
- Cultural stereotypes (Guide #4)
- Patterns of understanding related to ecological conditions (Guide #5)
- Nonverbal communication (Guide #8)
- Classroom orchestration (Guide #9)
- Gender bias (Guide #10)
- Student participation (Guide #11)

PRIMARY SOCIALIZATION

As we use the phrase here, primary socialization refers to the complex and often overlooked process of communication whereby a person (student) acquires from a significant other (teacher) ways in which to think and talk about the social world. It is generally a dependency relationship, in that the student is encountering many aspects of culture at a conceptual level for the first time. However, not all classroom communication involves primary socialization. If students lack a shared background of cultural experience or have already learned from different "significant others" (peers, parents, etc.), the explanations provided by the teacher may not have an influence on the students. We shall focus on the gatekeeper role teachers play as they introduce knowledge when the student views the teacher as a "significant other," encounters some aspect of culture for the first time, and shares enough of a common cultural background to participate in meaningful ways. The dynamics of primary socialization occur simultaneously, but in order to illuminate the critical areas of professional judgment, we have identified three distinct aspects of this process.

Complexity of Language

As language provides a schema or conceptual map for thinking, the initial vocabulary and theoretical framework made available to students serves as the initial conceptual scaffolding for understanding. In effect the language made available by the teacher or textbook introduces the student to the language community's way of thinking—though this does not exclude the possibility of misinterpretation on the teacher's or student's part, or of adopting at a later time a different way of thinking. The process of encountering the language essential for initial thoughts about some area of the cultural world (how to think about work, scientific method, community, technology, natural resources, and so forth) involves a number of professional judgments on the teacher's part. If teachers are not clear about this process, they are likely to make unconscious decisions that too often have the effect of leaving students with a language framework that is inadequate for understanding the complexity of the culture they are learning to think about. Thus the following questions can serve as a guide for insuring that the student's initial basis of understanding can lead to the development of further communicative competence:

Does the complexity of the vocabulary match the complexity of the culture the student is supposed to "understand"? For example, describing the brain as "like a computer" or the natural environment as "a resource" represents both an oversimplification and a narrow conceptual framework.

Is the language framework appropriate to the background experience and
maturity of the students?

Does the framework force students to understand a new abstraction in terms
of previously learned abstractions?

Do the analogues (models, examples, sources of comparison) used for introducing a new concept reflect hidden gender or cultural biases that will
exclude or alienate some students?

The emphasis in schools on learning how to think about different aspects of the
culture gives the teacher a great deal of power over the language-schemata ac-
quisition process of students. These questions thus serve to identify some of the
more critical moments in this dependency relationship.

Making Taken-for-Granted Beliefs Explicit

Taken-for-granted knowledge is a large part of the background that students, teachers, and authors who develop curriculum materials bring to their part
in the process of primary socialization. Because this tacit knowledge influences
both what and how learning occurs—for all participants—it is necessary for
teachers to be aware of the professional judgments associated with this aspect of
culture. These judgments, which have to do with knowing when to make explicit
the taken-for-granted beliefs, involve being sensitive to the taken-for-granted assumptions and patterns of thought embedded in curriculum materials, the
thought and communication processes of students, and, in terms of the most difficult of all to recognize, the teacher's own body of knowledge. As not all taken-
for-granted beliefs can or should be made explicit, the teacher's professional
judgment is made even more critical. In some instances the teacher must keep
up with the social reconstituting of taken-for-granted knowledge, and in other
instances (e.g., in areas relating to the cultural roots of the ecological crisis) the
teacher should take a leadership role that can only be fulfilled by modeling and
not simply by substituting a new set of taken-for-granted beliefs for the older
ones.

Historical and Cross-Cultural Perspectives

Introducing new knowledge often presents the danger that the knowledge
will be represented as objective and thus universally true. If we take seriously
the manner in which language provides schemata for thinking, we can see that
knowledge—even when represented as "objective information" and "factual"—
is an interpretation that reflects the conceptual categories and taken-for-granted
assumptions of the language community that creates it. Put another way, observation and thinking are not like a camera that re-presents the external world;

rather they are processes influenced by interpretative schemata encoded in the metaphorical nature of language. While we may lose sight of the interpretative aspects of knowledge (over time it tends to become part of shared taken-for-granted knowledge), there are critical moments in the process of primary socialization when the teacher needs to introduce a historical and/or a cross-cultural perspective in order for students to recognize that otherwise objective information, facts, and knowledge all have human authorship. Historical and cross-cultural perspectives provide an opportunity to clarify the patterns of thought and assumptions that are encoded in the "facts," and the historical perspective also offers an opportunity to identify continuities between past and present.

METAPHORICAL BASIS OF THOUGHT

It is rare in any classroom for a new concept or skill to be introduced without the use of metaphor. The reason for this is that new ideas are not easily understood on their own terms. Rather, understanding most easily takes place when students are able to make comparisons with some area of experience or concept with which they are already familiar. Explaining the nature of the human genome in a biology class, for example, is made easier through the use of a book analogy (metaphor), which is familiar to students. Consider a teacher's explanation: "You can think of exons as if they are parts of the paragraphs (genes) that specify various genetic functions. These paragraphs (genes) are organized into chapters, which are groups of DNA molecules called chromosomes. And the 'book' of the human genome can be thought of as consisting of two, nearly identical, volumes of 23 chapters (chromosomes) each." Even explanations of less difficult concepts are more easily understood when the teacher suggests a comparison with what is already familiar to students. Phrases and words such as "as if," "as like," "compare" are such a common aspect of the teacher's explanations that they largely go unnoticed. The use of these phrases and words signals the use of metaphor as an integral part of the teaching-learning process. But often the presence of metaphorical thinking is not signaled explicitly. An explanation of the human body as consisting of "parts," a book titled *The Uprooted*, and a reference to "behavioral outcomes" are also examples of metaphorical thinking, but in these cases the students may not be alerted by the use of the "as if" or "as like" phrases that one concept or type of activity is being understood in comparison with another, different concept or activity.

Because language and thought are dependent on metaphor, and because metaphors are usually taken for granted, we want to identify three categories of metaphorical thinking that will help in recognizing how the teacher orchestrates this aspect of the mental ecology of the classroom. These three categories overlap, but they are still useful in alerting us to the scope of metaphors and the variety of contexts in which they hold educational importance.

Analogic Thinking

Our comments above have been primarily about the use of analogic thinking where a familiar concept or experience is used as a basis of understanding new concepts. The familiar (e.g., the organization of books, the nature of a game, the characteristics of a machine, and so forth) provides a known pattern. That is, the analogue can be understood as a schema, model, or interpretative framework (all three being used here as interchangeable) for thinking about the new concept. It offers, in effect, the initial basis of new understandings and thus can be viewed as a generative metaphor. The use of the familiar to understand the unfamiliar can be a real test of the teacher's professional judgment, particularly when students, in encountering a new concept, are heavily dependent upon the language made available to them as part of the process of primary socialization. If they are being told to think of the body as having parts and functions they may not be aware that the generative metaphor of a machine may be inappropriate for understanding a living organism. That is, the generative metaphor that provides the initial schema or model of understanding may be inappropriate—like thinking of the classroom in terms of a factory, politics as like a sporting event, and the earth as a resource for humans to use.

Thinking of something as like something else highlights the similarities but not the differences between two domains of experience. Yet the differences that are put out of focus by the metaphor may be as important as the similarities when it comes to gaining a more in-depth understanding. Teachers may therefore need to give special attention to the dissimilarities or conceptual boundaries of instructional metaphors. Students may also lose sight of the "as if" aspect of metaphorical thinking, and base thought and action on a literal interpretation of a metaphorical construct. Addressing this situation again requires sensitivity on the teacher's part to how metaphor provides a basis for cultural understandings.

Still another question related to the teacher's professional judgments concerns whether the process of analogic thinking provides all students in the classroom with a common reference point for understanding the new concept. The familiar experiences and conceptual understandings that are to serve as the analogue (model) for establishing a basis of new understanding may be age, gender, ethnic, and/or social class specific.

Iconic Metaphors

Iconic metaphors are image words that encode earlier stages of analogic thinking. In effect, they reproduce ways of understanding worked out in the past. When students learn to think with iconic metaphors, their thought process is often unconsciously influenced by the mental processes encoded in the iconic metaphor. Since iconic metaphors, like analogic metaphors, are generally taken for granted, both the teacher and students often come under the control of a thought pattern of which they may not be aware. Examples of iconic metaphors that are now recognized as encoding the thought process of an earlier period, which was influenced by the prevailing cultural assumptions and social problems of that time, include "mankind," "intelligence," "traditions," "equality," "modernization," "work," "individualism," and so forth. The unrecognized iconic metaphors we use are as pervasive as the images we string together to make up sentences. For example, the following sentence (taken from a textbook) is typical in terms of the use of taken-for-granted image words: "*Humans stand at the top of the scale of complexity*" (the iconic metaphors are italicized).

Professional judgments in teaching should include recognizing when an iconic metaphor encodes a pattern of thought that is now considered outmoded or problematic in the sense that it needs to be made explicit and reexamined. Examples include "mankind," "progress," "success," "community," "creativity," "art," "science," and so forth. Professional decisions also surround the issue of knowing when iconic metaphors need to be put in historical perspective: What were the problems that people were facing when they worked out that particular way of thinking? What served as the analogue of their understanding? How were they influenced by their past? What were the cultural and gender-related assumptions they took for granted?

Root Metaphors

Thinking is also dependent upon the use of *root* metaphors, which help generate a particular way of understanding but are more deeply embedded in the collective consciousness of a language community than are analogic metaphors. Examples of root metaphors that we can now recognize include the idea of original sin, a view of the universe as a machine, and the image of a human-(man-) centered world. Root metaphors can thus be understood as themes, paradigms, or world views. They influence the process of analogic thinking and, over time, generate iconic metaphors that are conceptually coherent because of their grounding in a common root metaphor. Because of the multiple influences on the development of American society, and the layering and interpenetration of root metaphors, this deep aspect of the thought process is more difficult to recognize and sort out. But there are times when the root metaphor is clearly discernable. It is in these moments that the teacher should be able to recognize the educational importance of making root metaphors explicit. This may involve helping students recognize the guiding influence of the root metaphor—like when textbooks represent the earth as a "resource," communities as made up solely of people, and rationality as the only form of intelligence (all examples of an anthropocentric view of the universe). There may be other instances when the teacher needs to introduce a cross-cultural perspective in order for students to recognize the deeply held models and narratives that frame how we view the nature of work, technology, time, competition, and so forth. The introduction of historical or cross-cultural perspectives is essentially a professional judgment that relates to the constitutive role that a root metaphor plays in the thought process. Again, the key implications for classroom teaching center on knowing when and how to make implicit knowledge explicit.

CULTURALLY STEREOTYPED PATTERNS OF THOUGHT AND VALUES

The technical orientation of many teacher education programs combined with the inherent difficulties in developing cultural awareness too often results in an insensitivity to the culturally stereotyped ideas and values in textbooks and other curriculum materials. The dominant orientation in teacher education programs is to view the student as an autonomous individual (that is, free of cultural influences), the content of the curriculum as factual information, and language as a neutral conduit through which factual information is "transmitted" or simply given to students. When culture—including metaphor and other forms of tacit knowledge—is taken into account, these guiding assumptions become themselves a clear example of a culturally stereotyped belief. Textbooks, software, and films (because they are part of the primary socialization process) often present the beliefs and values of the dominant cultural group as if these were normal ("the same") for everybody. Examples of stereotyped cultural beliefs and values that are often represented to students as universals that every modern person takes for granted include: how competition leads to individual success and social betterment, the authority of individual judgment, a view of technology as politically and morally neutral (but also as the engine of progress), and the progressive nature of change. These iconic metaphors—competition, individualism, technology, and change, to stay with the examples just cited—encode the earlier thought processes of a specific cultural group as its members met what were perceived to be the challenges and sense of purpose of their times.

Classrooms are increasingly made up of students from a variety of cultural backgrounds, and teachers cannot simply assume that all students share the presuppositions held by the dominant cultural group. Thus, the teacher must continually be alert to the cultural orientation that is being represented to students as the normal way of thinking. In effect, the cultural content of the curriculum is a critical area of professional decision making. The challenge lies in knowing how to put the beliefs and values of the dominant culture into a perspective that is accessible to all students while encouraging students from other cultural backgrounds not to devalue their own traditions.

PATTERNS OF THOUGHT RELATED TO
AN ECOLOGICAL AWARENESS

The near daily reports on the environmentally disruptive consequences of our cultural practices suggest another area in which the teacher's professional judgment plays a critical role. Many teachers have already become sensitive to the often subtle ways in which racist and sexist beliefs are embedded in curriculum materials, so the idea that they have a responsibility for helping to insure that the beliefs and practices passed on to youth will not contribute to the further deterioration of the life-sustaining capacity of the ecosystem has precedents in the responsibilities they have assumed in the past. The teacher's professional judgments relate foremost to understanding how cultural beliefs and values, formed in the distant past in response to a different set of circumstances, become encoded in the language of the curriculum. The metaphors of community, technology, resource, progress, and so forth, encode the schema or thought pattern of an earlier time when the scale of the environment in relation to human activity seemed limitless. The image of community, for example, referred to a group of people (sometimes viewed as interdependent) living together within a definable space, but it did not include nonhuman forms of life. Similarly, the schema for thinking about progress, often associated with technological advances and higher levels of consumerism, does not take into account how the social practices based on this way of thinking are depleting nonrenewable resources. We could easily cite other examples of how dominant belief systems not only contribute to the ecological crisis, but also obstruct understanding the connections between cultural practices and the deterioration of the earth's life-sustaining capabilities. The challenge for the teacher is to be alert to the presence of beliefs, assumptions, and values that are now being made problematic by our increasing knowledge of the scale of ecological damage. Again, this includes knowing when to bring forward historical or cross-cultural perspectives, thus making explicit taken-for-granted assumptions about ecological conditions.

NONVERBAL COMMUNICATION

We often use the term *behavior* to describe individual physical performance, such as when we refer to a student's "off-task behavior." This conventional view of behavior, unfortunately, tends to hide the most educationally important dimension of classroom behavior, namely that it is a way of signalling attitudes about interpersonal relationships through a variety of nonverbal channels. Simply stated, behavior is another form of communication, and since much of a student's behavior follows patterns shared by members of a cultural group, it can also be understood as a powerful form of language. "Actions speak louder than words."

Gregory Bateson refers to communication about relationships as *metacommunication,* and he argues that this dimension of information exchange influences how participants will respond to a spoken message. Body posture, the use of one's eyes, gaze, tone of voice, pausing, spatial distance, and so forth represent, in effect, supplemental messages that the participants communicate to each other. Compared with spoken messages, nonverbal messages comment more directly on interpersonal relationships and often become more important to understanding than the content of the verbal message. "It's the way you said it" or "I thought you weren't listening" are really references to how behavior can be seen as communicating a message that drowns out everything else.

Sitting in the back row of a classroom or turning one's gaze toward the window or ceiling while speaking to another person—to cite two very different examples—communicate messages that people within the dominant Anglo culture will understand in essentially the same way. This is true because behavior, to a larger extent than is commonly recognized, derives its meaning from culturally shared patterns. Students from cultural backgrounds that are different from that of the teacher may thus use taken-for-granted communication patterns that are not understood by the teacher in the way they were intended.

When behavior is seen as a language system, the task of interpreting what the student's behavior means becomes extremely complex. Nevertheless, it is a task that the teacher cannot ignore if communication in increasingly multicultural classrooms is to facilitate the type of interpersonal relationships essential to education. Ignoring how a smile, eye contact, silence, and so forth may reflect cultural differences can contribute to misunderstandings and alienating relationships. The teacher's professional judgments are made even more complicated when we recognize that judging students solely on the basis of perceived connections between a pattern and a cultural group may lead to stereotyping.

There are three channels of nonverbal communication that may involve cultural differences: proxemics, kinesics, and prosody. *Proxemics* has to do with how the use of space (seen as a behavior) is used to communicate about relationships. Where the teacher stands within the classroom signals different messages, for example, just as the student who sits in the back of the classroom sends a different message than the student who sits up front, where eye contact can be established with the teacher and where head nodding integrates the student into the rhythm of class activities (and is seen by the teacher). *Kinesics* includes what is more popularly known as body language—the use of eyes, gaze, movement of hands, and body posture. Body movement and gestures, it has been found, are synchronized with the rhythm (itself a culturally specific pattern) of speaking—including the taking of turns and the status relationship between speaker and listener. *Prosody* involves the signals and cues communicated through the changes in voice tone, pitch, inflection, and rhythm (including pauses).

Understanding how the use of these nonverbal channels is influenced by the primary cultural affiliations of teachers and students is something that cannot be learned simply from a textbook. Instead, teachers must learn to work in a receptive mode, open to recognizing the students' and their own taken-for-granted patterns of nonverbal communication. *Responsive Teaching* (1990) further summarizes the range of cultural differences that can be found in most classrooms and suggests concrete steps teachers can take in recognizing and responding to different patterns. The supervision guides in the back of this manual also identify a number of nonverbal patterns that have been found to be critically important in fostering a positive learning environment for students. However, it must be acknowledged that this dimension of professional judgment cannot be laid out in advance like a recipe; it is a matter that requires an understanding of context and culture.

ORCHESTRATION OF STUDENT INVOLVEMENT

The teacher exercises control over a number of classroom processes that have an influence on the students' perception of how they are to be involved in the learning process. The ability to exercise this control is, to a certain degree, reinforced by the conventional regard for the teacher's role, but the expectations that accompany that role do not guarantee that students will passively accept being controlled or that the classroom atmosphere will be conducive to learning. In short, the teacher cannot succeed without the support of the students, and this requires that the teacher's approach to control take the form of orchestrating student involvement in a manner that is recognized (by students) as fair and supportive.

The Role of Framing in Communication

Framing is a term used to describe one of the most fundamental aspects of communication, but the dynamic nature of the process makes it difficult to isolate and define. Basically, framing involves separating an activity or process from the surrounding flow of events: The activities that are to be attended to are, in effect, contained within the frame. This provides for focused activities. A whistle, for example, signals a change in the frame from "time out" to the resumption of the game, and thus a change in what is to be attended to as well as the appropriate patterns of involvement. Similarly, the classroom buzzer and the closing of the door both signal a change of frame, and it is assumed that all the participants understand the behavior and role relationships appropriate to the new "lesson" frame. Conversations also require framing; otherwise, the participants would be attempting to communicate without a shared sense of how they are to be involved and what the focus of the conversation is about. The subtle nature of framing in a conversation can be seen in how changes in tone of voice, body gestures, and so forth may cause a shift in frames—along with mood and patterns of involvement—so that a serious topic is reframed into a joking situation, which in turn is transformed by another metacommunication pattern (one of the participants glances at her watch) into the obligatory farewell remarks. The term "footing" refers to establishing a common understanding of how participants are to relate to each other in dealing with the activity that has been framed. The student who says to the teacher, "Not bad for your first day," is using a footing (communicating a relationship) that changes what was initially being framed as a compliment into a message that suggests confusion (and possibly trouble ahead) about their social status.

Effective teaching requires communication skills that will help all students recognize the activity being framed and the footing appropriate for participation. At times it may be necessary for the teacher to name the frame (that is, make it explicit) in order to insure that student comments do not take the conversation off in directions inappropriate at that point in the learning process. Negotiation over frames is always an aspect of classroom conversation, and this also requires a sensitivity to the possibility that a comment or question from a student may establish a new and unanticipated frame that is educationally significant. Knowing when in the course of a class discussion to return to the main curricular themes also requires that the teacher recognize that this task of reframing requires conscious direction, as well as skill in acknowledging previous student contributions.

Turn-Taking and Negotiation

The social ecology of the classroom is also affected by how the teacher orchestrates the allocation of speaking turns and handles assignments and the rules that are to guide student performance. The way these tasks are carried out can establish a footing that influences the educational significance of an activity—whether, for example, the students perceive their involvement as active or passive. This, in turn, will influence whether students perceive the teacher as fair and unbiased. If turns to speak are granted primarily to students who are viewed as achievers or in agreement with the teacher's personal point of view, a division will likely emerge within the class, and achievement will become increasingly restricted to a particular group. Distributing the allocation of speaking turns evenly throughout the class, on the other hand, sends a different message about what and whom the teacher values.

Although nearly every aspect of classroom life requires student involvement, if not active support, it is possible for the teacher to lose sight of the interdependent nature of the classroom ecology. When this occurs the teacher may dictate assignments and behavioral expectations in a closed communication style. One teacher aptly described the mindset that often gives rise to this situation: "I came in with the idea that this is *my* classroom and *you* [the student] conform to the rules." The reaction to closed communication, depending on grade level, may range from increasing passivity and alienation to overt acts of resistance. A negotiating style of classroom leadership does not mean that power is shared equally with students, but it does recognize—and communicate to students—that expectations about assignments and classroom performance are based on an understanding of the other pressures that students are experiencing. It also takes account of the connection between motivation and opportunities for meaningful participation in the decision-making process.

Power and Solidarity in the Classroom

The classroom, as we have been suggesting in the previous discussion, involves both the exercise of power (which is expressed in the teacher's control and direction of classroom activities) and the achievement of solidarity through feelings of shared interest, rapport, caring, mutual respect, and interdependency. Teaching involves knowing where classroom relationships fall on the power-solidarity continuum, and whether they are appropriate to an educational context. Teachers may strengthen solidarity through the use of humor, by not taking themselves too seriously, through dialogue, by encouraging student participation, and through caring. A more problematic sense of solidarity may also be created if the teacher befriends a few special students exclusively or sends out messages that promote the weak illusion of an egalitarian atmosphere. If the teacher then moves more to the power end of the continuum when it is necessary to make pedagogical decisions that students may not have the maturity and judgment to fully understand, students can feel that the teacher has betrayed a personal relationship, as reflected in such comments as: "If the teacher was really my friend why can't she accept the answer I want to give?" or "How could he give me that grade?" In contrast, power may be utilized in some circumstances to promote a sense of solidarity, such as when a student comments, "I like that teacher because she forces me to think." Maintaining a balance between the exercise of power (authority) and achieving solidarity requires a sensitivity to changes in the classroom ecology—which means recognizing cultural patterns and orchestrating with a light touch.

GENDER BIAS

The assumptions and patterns of a culture are encoded in our everyday habits—including speech, nonverbal communication, perception, and what is experienced as rewarding. Although awareness of gender bias in the classroom has increased, we seem to be in a transition period in which past habits of making gender distinctions in the treatment of students still occur in some classrooms. Patterns of differential treatment (experienced at a taken-for-granted level) may be expressed in a variety of ways, but the following appear to be the most prevalent:

1. Uses of language in ways that privilege the masculine over the feminine (e.g., "he," "you guys," "mankind," etc.)
2. The use of analogues—stories, examples, metaphors, and visual illustrations—that are derived essentially from areas of experience traditionally perceived as masculine
3. Fostering an atmosphere of competitive individualism where achievers are recognized and the noncompetitive students are disadvantaged
4. Various uses of humor that may include dismissing the contributions of female students, treating them as the object of the joke, and maintaining a teasing relationship that has sexual overtones
5. Granting more speaking turns to male students as well as following up male student contributions with additional comments that highlight their importance while adopting a more passive form of response to the contributions of female students

As the self-identity of students (including their sense of self-worth and competence) is especially vulnerable when they are learning something new (including who they are in relation to the new knowledge or skill), it is critical that the traditional cultural biases in the area of gender not be reproduced as part of student learning. Past experience has taught us that such gender biases inhibit personal development by fostering self-doubt; they may also strengthen the student's own taken-for-granted gender stereotypes. With students who are sensitive to this problem, the expression of bias on the teacher's part—even when it occurs unconsciously—will contribute to a loss of respect and, in some instances, to a confrontational relationship.

CULTURALLY APPROPRIATE PARTICIPATION PATTERNS

The organization of classroom learning and the patterns of interaction among its participants are never culturally neutral. The physical layout of the

classroom itself expresses the ideas of a culture. Students learning to study under the direction of a teacher, to work alone and in competition with others, and
to accept linear patterns where print and numbers are given special recognition
as sources of authority, are undergoing a process of acculturation—in this case,
to the patterns that are taken for granted by dominant Anglo groups. Even the
practice of treating the student as an autonomous individual whose rationality is
dependent upon "objectivity" expresses a specific cultural point of view. This
way of viewing the student represents stereotyped thinking that may often pre-
vent the teacher from recognizing the patterns—of social interaction, thought,
knowledge, and authority—that characterize the student's primary culture.
There is also the danger of stereotyping the student (and teacher) in terms of
skin color or physical characteristics, clothes, and other attributes that are sometimes used as a basis for judgment. With the growing interaction of cultural
groups, including the influences of the media, students may identify with a variety of cultural groups, or they may have become enculturated to the patterns and
natural attitudes of the dominant Anglo culture. The task of the teacher is
twofold: (1) to recognize that the patterns of interaction taken for granted within
the dominant culture are not universally shared, and (2) to become aware of the
patterns with which students most easily identify. Because so much depends
upon context (including the cultural background of each student), we can only
provide general guidelines for becoming more responsive to the appropriateness
of the participation patterns used to organize student-teacher interaction.

Participation patterns vary quite widely, but of particular concern is that the
individualistic, competitive, and teacher-centered patterns of Anglo cultural
groups appear to conflict with the participation patterns of many non-Western
groups. In some, where childrearing is shared widely within the community,
knowledge and guidance are not acquired from a single adult. There may also be
more emphasis on group interaction and sharing. In some instances researchers
have found that when the teacher changes the participation patterns of the classroom to include more opportunities for group work and more emphasis on cooperation than on spotlighting individual successes, students become more fully
involved. Moreover, recognizing that narrative forms of knowledge may be
more meaningful for some students than learning the abstract knowledge that is
characteristic of print-oriented communication can lead to changes, such as ad-
justing the curriculum to include the community bearers of traditional knowledge.

Because even the body language of the student signals cultural membership,
it is important that the teacher become familiar with the cultural patterns being
re-enacted by students as part of their classroom interaction, while at the same
time recognizing the participation patterns and socio-spatial organization that
the teacher takes for granted.

CHAPTER 3

How to Use This Handbook

Our emphasis on *cultural* responsiveness—the grounding of professional practice on a recognition of patterns that would otherwise be taken for granted—both distinguishes our approach and focuses it on such topics as metaphor, body language, turn-taking, humor, gender bias, and framing. These topics are useful in addressing the cultural dimensions of teaching. At the same time, they require that we reconceptualize supervision as a form of qualitative inquiry—one that is sensitive to the contextual and interpretive nature of culture.

In practical terms, this means that our approach will *not* offer supervisors a set of "instruments" (behavioral checklists, rating scales, or "low-inference" observation schedules). Such tools have a place in particular approaches to educational research, but even the most sophisticated are able to capture only an exceedingly thin slice of what it means to teach.

What we will offer is a vocabulary, in the form of eleven illustrated observation guides. These guides are intended to serve as memory aids during the process of supervision. Each belongs to one of two major categories: the "mental" (Guides 1–7) or "social" (Guides 8–11) ecology of the classroom. Although these categories overlap broadly, we have found them useful in suggesting two basic questions relevant to the significance of classroom observations. First, how can these observations (as examples of teaching) be understood in terms of what the students are learning (i.e., the mental ecology or the nature of ideas conveyed in the classroom)? Second, how can these observations be understood in terms of student-teacher relationships (the social ecology of the classroom)? Again, our experience suggests that most observations can be related to both the mental and social ecologies of teaching, but that raising the question at an explicit level helps direct attention to the more specific concerns of *how* an observation is related to each context.

Beyond these broad parameters, we will make recommendations for using the observation guides at various stages in what, with some modification, has come to be known as a supervision cycle. The stages include:

1. Pre-observation conferencing
2. Classroom observations
3. Review of fieldnotes
4. Feedback conferencing

PRE-OBSERVATION CONFERENCING

From the supervisor's perspective, initial meetings and discussions with a teacher are critically important for two reasons. First, they provide an opportunity for supervisors to begin their observations, asking questions and taking note of background information relevant to the teacher's assumptions and cultural presuppositions about the nature of teaching. The supervisor's initial receptivity to the teacher's point of view often helps avoid teacher-supervisor miscommunication at later stages. In effect, culturally responsive supervision involves being sensitive to the same cultural patterns in the supervisor-teacher relationship as exist in the teacher-student relationship, and the guides for observing those patterns in the classroom are therefore also applicable to the supervisor-teacher conference. What metaphors, for example, do teachers use in describing their work? On what traditions and values are these metaphors grounded? What is communicated, especially about the teacher-supervisor relationship, by body language, the use of space, and tone of voice? Are these nonverbal messages culturally specific? How do teachers and supervisors manage to frame these initial meetings? What types of humor could be used to promote solidarity? Will the use of technical words be viewed as an expression of power?

Pre-observation conferencing also provides an opportunity for the supervisor and teacher to discuss the anticipated focus of classroom observations. The question of focus is critical. Qualitative researchers have approached it in a number of different ways. On one side of the issue, we have already argued that the prespecification of focus (e.g., behavioral checklists and rating scales) often obscures rather than highlights the most significant aspects of teaching. We are also concerned that such procedures send messages to teachers that their work is narrowly conceived by the supervisor. On the other side of the issue, supervisors cannot (even if it were desirable) come to their work "empty headed." Our observation guides are intended to accommodate both concerns by providing a rich vocabulary—one that underscores the multiple dimensions of language and learning without an overly strict specification of "what counts." In communicating this stance, supervisors may well wish to share the observation guides with teachers, or provide some type of overview of their content, making clear that the guides encompass far more than could be addressed even over a lengthy period of supervision.

Some authors may argue that teachers and *not* supervisors should take responsibility for deciding the focus of supervision. From this perspective, the supervisor is viewed as being a "problem-solver" whose duties lie in bringing professional skills to whatever the teacher has defined as a difficulty or source of trouble. Yet we would argue that if the process is to be genuinely helpful to teachers, the supervisor must be willing to assist them in formulating as well as in solving problems. The reason for this concerns a point we previously emphasized regarding the taken-for-granted nature of cultural knowledge. Because most of our knowledge (about teaching, students, the curriculum, etc.) is implicit, we often require a third-party perspective in order to gain fresh insights into what we and others take for granted. Reflection alone simply does not provide for the types of learning that we hope teachers will model. We are suggesting that the supervisor's professional responsibilities include providing leadership when it comes to defining the scope and content of supervision. Our observation guides are designed to offer a set of frameworks for addressing this task.

CLASSROOM OBSERVATIONS

We have just argued that supervisors should provide some degree of leadership in directing the course of supervision. Yet we still view their work as requiring a great deal of receptivity. Our handbook begins with the suggestion that observation lies at the very heart of supervision. Like others engaged in forms of qualitative inquiry, the supervisor goes into the field in order to learn about the particulars of a classroom, teacher, lesson, school day, and so forth. The work of supervisors has traditionally been tied more explicitly and directly to school improvement than has, for example, that of ethnographers, but both must strive toward a heightened perception of cultural patterns that will afford them insight into what they have observed.

Thus one of the central challenges of responsive supervision lies in developing an ability to "read" the interpretive, emergent, and often subtle dimensions of social interactions that characterize school experience. For this reason, responsive supervisors (again, like qualitative researchers) do not go into a classroom with the sole purpose of counting the number of times a teacher engages in a particular behavior. Such techniques may play a part in supervision, but they should never be allowed to divorce behavior from the socio-cultural contexts that give it meaning. In short, we view observation as a skill that must be achieved rather than prescribed.

But then how, exactly, are observations achieved? The ethnographer's fieldwork is guided by conventions that define anthropology. Supervisors may borrow more freely from a variety of disciplines, but they too must rely on the broader purposes of their field, in this case education. As we have already argued, these broader purposes are concerned foremost with fostering cultural awareness and the ability to fully participate in cultural processes of renewal. The observation guides we have developed are closely aligned with these concerns. They are intended to be used in conjunction with fieldnotes in which the supervisor records ongoing events as well as observational themes. Although the guides are designed for quick reference and the handbook itself is small enough to be carried into the classroom as part of an observation notebook, a supervisor need not always consult the guides during an observation. Some supervisors, for example, may wish to review certain guides only immediately before or after a period of observation in order to remind them of either specific topics (e.g., the use of space in the classroom, gender-biased metaphors, patterns of turn-taking that support cooperation, etc.) or the relationships between topics (e.g., the use of space as a dimension of primary socialization). Other supervisors may refer to guides during their observations, but only when they sense that their field-notes are becoming disjointed or superficial. After supervisors have gained experience in recognizing patterns of tacit, cultural knowledge (e.g., metaphor, nonverbal communication, framing, etc.), they may refer to the observation guides less and less frequently. In any case, the guides are designed to be used with a good deal of flexibility.

REVIEW

The supervision cycle is often described as moving from classroom observations directly to some form of post-observation conference in which the supervisor can provide feedback and possibly make recommendations for improving the teacher's instructional performance. We would like to suggest an intervening stage during which our observation guides could again inform supervisory practices. This "review" stage would allow supervisors an opportunity to go back over their fieldnotes in order to develop themes that can help explain what they have observed and to synthesize the educational significance of those observations. After they have made observations, supervisors are left with field-notes that represent a focused yet still broadly based collection of examples, illustrations, and descriptions. The significance of a particular description, however, may not be immediately apparent even when it is a salient dimension of the teacher's daily instruction. Here the observation guides can be used not so much in order to provide focus (as suggested earlier), but rather to situate a description or example within a framework that lends it both meaning and significance.

Consider the following illustration. A supervisor observes (and records) several instances where the teacher openly questions or calls attention to the presuppositions upon which the curriculum materials are based. The following quotes by the teacher, for example, are recorded in the supervisor's fieldnotes: "I'm going to read the chapter summary aloud, but let's see if you can recognize anything important the authors have left out," "This introduction gives six examples of famous scientists, and they're all men; why do you think that's the case?" "The book says that scientists believe the earth to be about 4.5 billion years old, but they haven't always believed that." Are these quotes important, and why? Are they worth more explicit consideration, or is some other aspect of this teacher's instruction more significant? In addressing such questions, the supervisor may wish to go back to the guides to see how these quotes relate, for example, to the general process of primary socialization. This process helps the supervisor link otherwise isolated examples to a variety of themes, such as how the teacher's comments frame a particular subject (in this case, science), whether the teacher provides students with a vocabulary that enables them to recognize the cultural grounding of knowledge, and whether the teacher is able to relate the curriculum to the students' experience. Again, such thematic analyses hinge on the supervisor's ability to recognize the otherwise hidden patterns of culture.

PROVIDING FEEDBACK

A post-observation conference is usually viewed as the primary context for providing teachers with feedback and recommendations. Within this context (and in some cases outside of it), feedback may take the form of either written or verbal reports. In both cases a culturally responsive approach to supervision holds a number of practical implications. Given that the supervisor's knowledge and insights are highly contextualized in this approach, written reports are likely to include a good deal of detailed description and narrative (they could, in some instances, be comprised wholly of brief vignettes). Such literary formats utilize expressive and figurative as well as propositional language. It is thus particularly important for supervisors to use the observation guides or a similar framework in monitoring how they provide feedback. For example, the guides call for close attention to metaphor, tone, and diction—the style as well as the message itself. Even such seemingly mundane concerns as the quality of paper used and whether a report is handwritten or typed help frame the message and thus influence the teacher-supervisor relationship. In the case of verbal reports similar concerns apply: tone (in its literal meaning), posture, the location of the conference (on whose turf?), patterns of turn-taking, pacing, the use of space (Is the supervisor or teacher "barricaded" behind a desk?), gestures, facial expressions, and dress. Again, all of these factors and how they are coordinated with a spoken message play into the complex task of framing social interaction. Tone, posture, use of space, and so forth communicate, and they are thus potentially significant in shaping what messages the teacher takes away from the exchange.

Finally, we want to reiterate our concerns regarding focus within the context of providing feedback. First, it should be clear that the supervisors would be mistaken in any attempt to "cover" all of the topics suggested by our observation guides. Simply as a matter of coherence and practical necessity, supervisors must be selective in what they choose to report, assessing information viewed as most significant in terms of the broader purposes of education. Second, we hope that our guides, in making particular domains of tacit knowledge explicit, will help move supervisors from providing general feedback ("You have a positive teaching style," or "You seem to get along well with your students") to more focused comments: "Your use of humor does not exclude anyone in the class and thus contributes to feelings of solidarity. For example,...." "Your nonverbal cues, especially how close you stand to the students and your body language, are well coordinated to signal that you're interested in what students have to say." These more focused comments are important not only because they are potentially informative, but because they communicate a sensitivity to the complexity of the ecology of the classroom.

Part II

Guides
for
Supervisors

The following guides suggest the range of patterns that are brought into focus by a culturally responsive approach to supervision. Below each numbered pattern we include one or more examples. These examples offer important illustrations of what to look for, but they do not exhaust the many possible forms that a given pattern might take within the context of a particular class.

Teaching often follows an identifiable structure. Although different approaches will influence the structural characteristics (or pattern) of the lesson, certain key elements are generally present. How students are to be involved often depends upon how the teacher frames the opening and closing of the lesson, communicates expectations for students, and makes adjustments in teaching style to match the flow of classroom events.

A. Introduction of the Lesson: Framing (establishing a common footing of understanding and participation)

1. Clear opening frame that establishes the purpose or context of the lesson
   - *Nonverbal:* Teacher rolls up shirt sleeves, takes position at center or front of room, raises voice, gestures, etc.
   - *Direct statement:* "Today's lesson is on photosynthesis"
   - *Metaphor:* "OK, let's get together"

2. Acknowledgment of how the main issues of previous lessons relate to current lesson
   - "In comparison," "as we saw before," "in contrast," "this lesson is related to," "connected with," "an example of," "useful for," etc.

3. Overview statements
   - *Direct:* "The theme of this lesson," "the main point," "the central concern," "the heart of this matter," etc.
   - *Providing a metaphor:* "This novel can be understood in terms of tension between...," "Equations are like a balance scale," "The stock market crash of 1929 was like a downward spiral."

4. Clarification of how students are expected to participate in the learning experience
   - *Direct:* "I will explain each concept; you give me an example." "Listen to your partners first, then summarize their comments."
   - *Metaphor:* "I'll act as 'guide,' 'coach,' 'partner,' 'critic,' etc." "You act as 'guide,' 'coach,' 'partner,' etc."

B. Teaching the Lesson: Matching Purpose of Lesson with Appropriate Teaching Style

1. Using appropriate examples to clarify concepts or to model performance
   - *Provides metaphor:* "You can think of a line as a single piece of string stretched tightly between two points."
   - *Models:* "Let me show you how to hold the racket."

2. Exploring student's way of understanding new concepts (including use of dialogue)

- *Questioning:* "How would you describe this book to a friend?"
- *Dialogue:* Students initiate comments, direct comments to other students, evaluate their own comments, acknowledge others, and self-select themselves as speakers

3. Attending to different dimensions of primary socialization process (language, tacit knowledge, and historical and cross-cultural perspectives)

- *Language/tacit knowledge:* "Why do we use the term *hard sciences?*" "...the term *Far East?*" "...the term *natural resources?*" etc.
- *Historical:* "How has this view changed over time?"
- *Cross-cultural:* "If we had grown up in a small fishing village, how might we see this...." "If we had grown up in the slums of New York," etc.

4. Sensitivity to cultural and gender differences among students

- *Providing alternative metaphors/frames:* "Let's try to think about art as both beautiful and useful, or as both individual and social, or as both...."
- *Making metaphor/pattern explicit:* "Why do we so often joke about X?" "Why is this difficult for us to understand?"

5. Orchestrating student participation in a manner that involves all students

- "Give me examples," "Do you have any questions," "Now it's your turn to explain, tell us, list, outline, etc."

C. Closure: Review and Providing for Continuity with Next Lesson

1. Clear summary of concepts that have been clarified, questions raised, and consensus achieved during lesson

- "What were the main questions, issues, agreements, or disagreements that came up today?"

2. Brief overview statements of how concepts and performances relate to next lessons

- "What we learned today we can use as a foundation, grounding, basis, platform, etc.," "This chapter sets the stage for...."

PRIMARY SOCIALIZATION

Primary socialization involves introducing students to new concepts or providing a basis (language, vocabulary, schema, etc.) for understanding some aspect of culture they have learned from previous experience. Culturally responsive supervision involves helping teachers understand how their decisions in this dynamic process influence understanding and the ability to recognize implicit cultural patterns.

A. **Control of Language (sharing of a conceptual schema): Complexity of Vocabulary**

   1. Adequately represents conceptual complexity of issue or aspect of experience

      • *Appropriate complexity:* Compare "The brain is like a computer (machine)" with "The brain is like a city (community)." Compare also "Government policy controls trade" with "In thinking about trade policies we can use at least three metaphors: interference, intervention, and protection."

   2. Avoids being overly abstract (clarifies vocabulary being used with examples or alternative vocabulary)

      • *Specific illustrations of abstract terms:* (From 4th grade science lesson on electricity) "What image do you have when you hear the word static? I think of a statue, like the bronze statue in front of the school."

   3. Uses vocabulary appropriate to maturity and cultural background of students

      • *Background- and age-appropriate vocabulary:* Teacher avoids language that reproduces cultural stereotypes (see also Guide #4).

   4. Establishes connections between vocabulary and student experience

      • *Experience based:* "Can you give me an example from your own experience?"

   5. Uses metaphors appropriate to gender and cultural differences (see Guide #3)

      • *Culture- and gender-appropriate metaphors:* Compare "Your examples are on target (or hit the mark)" with "Your examples clarify (or demonstrate)..." (see also Guide #3).

B. Making Taken-for-Granted (TFG) Beliefs Explicit

1. Recognizes TFG beliefs and attitudes in curriculum material

   • Teacher calls attention to assumptions or presuppositions of textbook author, filmmaker, etc.: "What does Chapter One imply about the relationship between science and tradition?"

2. Recognizes TFG beliefs in class discussion

   • Teacher calls attention to assumptions or presuppositions of student beliefs: "Why do we connect understanding with the ability to see, as in terms like *insight* and *vision*?"

3. Recognizes teacher's own TFG beliefs that are unconsciously shared

   • Teacher calls attention to his or her own assumptions or presuppositions: "I was taught to focus on the story and writing style, so I sometimes forget to consider the time and place in which the author lived."

4. Recognizes TFG beliefs that communicate gender, age, or ethnic biases

   • Teacher calls attention to implications/importance of assumed knowledge: "If we can only see this as a matter of business, then it's difficult to recognize the family's concern...."

C. Putting "Facts" in Historical Perspective

1. Avoids leaving students with reified knowledge (knowledge that is represented as objective, factual, etc.)

   • Teacher avoids pronouncements and declarative statements.

2. Introduces a historical perspective (social origin of knowledge, facts, etc.)

   • *Providing historical context:* "Where did this idea come from? What were some of the relevant concerns of that time?"

3. Introduces a cross-cultural perspective (i.e., how other cultural groups would interpret issues, events, "facts," etc.)

   • *Providing a cross-cultural perspective:* "In asking about how we understand what it means to be an artist (or successful, intelligent, literate, a woman, man, son, daughter, etc.) let me tell you a Chinese folk tale, ... an Indian proverb, ... a Brazilian poem," etc.

GUIDE #3:
THE METAPHORICAL BASIS OF THOUGHT

Robert Frost believed that every teacher's understanding of language should include a sense of when metaphors are likely to provide a basis for new insight
and when they are likely to break down. Understanding a new concept or experience often depends on our ability to relate it in some way to familiar experience. This is the essence of metaphorical thinking. In addition to this compara-
tive process that we call analogic thinking, iconic metaphor highlights how language connects our knowledge to historical patterns, and root metaphors bring
into focus how words provide ready-made conceptual schemata.

A. **Use of Analogic Metaphor in Introducing New Concepts Analogic
Thinking (understanding the new in terms of the familiar)**

1. Avoids inappropriate generative metaphor (e.g., comparing organic with
mechanical process)

   • Mind as "computer," mental fatigue as "burnout," curriculum as "in-
   put," and student behavior as "output" (based on student-as-machine
   metaphor), etc.

2. Explains the dissimilarities between what is being compared

   • "We say that the heart is like a pump, but unlike a pump your heart is
   part of a living organism, and is affected by your lifestyle, your daily
   routines, etc."

3. Calls attention to the "as if" dimension of metaphorical thinking

   • "When we say that these words convey ideas, what happens is not quite
   the same as me handing you a pencil, or chair, or piece of paper."

4. Insures relevance of generative metaphor (reference point for understanding new concept) to student experience

   • The president as quarterback, the bottom line, and social experiment
   assume some understanding/appreciation of football, business, and
   science.

5. Displays sensitivity to cultural or gender bias contained in generative
metaphors

   • Examples of gender biased metaphors include "the hard sciences," "on
   target" (note also those above: the president as quarterback, the bottom
   line, and social experiment), etc. (see also Guide #10).

B. Role of Iconic Metaphor in Reproducing Past Ways of Understanding

1. Calls attention to iconic metaphors that encode a pattern or schema for thinking that is now outmoded

   • Intelligence as IQ (culture-free), change as progress, the individual or species as unit of survival, the environment as resource (see also Guide #5).

2. Places iconic metaphor in historical context

   • "The ability to read in early America and in European countries was long associated with spiritual and religious life."

3. Is sensitive to how iconic metaphor encodes a culture- or gender-specific way of thinking

   • "Does this person define maturity in terms of independence," "learning in terms of individual achievement," "science as politically neutral," "language as a tool," etc.

C. Making Root Metaphors Explicit as Cultural World Views or Paradigms

1. Explains how patterns of thinking, including taken-for-granted assumptions, are grounded in a root metaphor

   • (From a high school English class) "The metaphor, *aesthetic distance* assumes that the writer can be separated or removed from the writing."

2. Introduces a cross-cultural comparison into discussion in order to make root metaphor explicit

   • "This group of people (culture) have different notions or understandings of art, ... leadership, ... economy, ... history," etc.

3. Uses root metaphors appropriate for understanding current problems

   • Urban blight is often used in ways that put out of focus community; genetic engineering in ways that put out of focus ethical issues; homework in ways that put out of focus intrinsic motivation.

GUIDE #4:
CULTURALLY STEREOTYPED PATTERNS
OF THOUGHT AND VALUES

Curriculum materials and classroom teaching always involve the transmission of distinct cultural ideas and values. These ideas and values are important because they provide a sense of coherence to our everyday experiences. Yet quite often they restrict our understanding of current social problems. Moreover, they may be inappropriate or insensitive to the primary culture of some students. Monitoring the transmission of these basic values, ideas, or attitudes is one of the central professional responsibilities of teachers.

Cultural Assumptions, Patterns of Thought, and Values That May Be Either Outmoded for All Students or Problematic In Terms of the Ethnic Composition of the Classroom:

1. Competition
   - Examples range from grading practices that ensure "winners" and "losers" to patterns of turn-taking where individual students must constantly bid against others for the teacher's attention.

2. Individualism
   - Again, a broad range of examples fit this category, from success being defined as individual achievement ("He won the game," "She got ahead by selling insurance on the weekends") to referencing the individual as a source of ideas ("What is her idea?") or activities ("Do your own work," "Don't copy from anyone else's paper.").

3. Technology as neutral
   - "The computer is a powerful tool," "Words give us an efficient way to communicate," "Technology is used in many industries."

4. Mechanistic view of environment, society, or person
   - "Your body, like a car, is made up of many complex parts" (from textbook), "That book turns me off," "Unless you study every day, you'll get rusty," "You need to get in gear this morning."

5. Change as progressive
   - "This new theory is much more advanced," "That group has always lagged behind, failing to keep pace with modern life," "Why cling to the past?"

6. Thought as data-based or data-driven
   - "Turn that information over in your mind," "You can't make an infor-

med decision unless you know the facts," "The first step in writing a paper is to gather information from the library."

7. Rational process as culture-free

   • "His logic was water-tight, but he often let his emotions get in the way," "You need to distance yourself from the situation in order to be objective." Examples would also include the failure to put words and ideas into a social-historical context.

8. Language as a conduit

   • Individual repeats a comment when not understood without revising it, or is impatient when not understood. Communication problems attributed to individual personality characteristics (lack of intelligence, hostility, aggression, etc.).

9. Success as individual achievement

   • "Not everyone can make it to the top," "It was a difficult campaign but he won the election," "You will get points for each assignment you do, and the number of points you earn determines your grade."

10. Work for money

    • "She is just a housewife, just a student, just a volunteer, etc."

11. Consumerism indicates success

    • "After his promotion he bought a large house," "Because her business was a success, she could afford luxuries."

12. Modernization viewed as progress

    • "This is the new, improved version," "We need some new, fresh ideas," "Modern science has revolutionized our world," etc.

13. Traditional cultures viewed as backward or unenlightened

    • Perspectives that presuppose the superiority of contemporary/modern cultures—"These nations have not yet developed an advanced economic system," "Tradition was the first barrier to the industrial revolution," "This writer, having a great deal of foresight, broke with tradition to establish a new genre."

14. Literate people viewed as more socially advanced

    • "Of course, he was embarrassed when they discovered he could not even write his name," "Whatever you write down, it must be your very best work," "She came from such a poor background that she could not even read or write."

PATTERNS OF THOUGHT RELATED TO
AN ECOLOGICAL AWARENESS

The language that constitutes curriculum and classroom instruction is grounded on assumptions and presuppositions that characterize the thought processes of the past. In many instances, past ways of thinking evolved in response to a very different set of social and environmental circumstances (e.g., vast continental frontiers) than what we now experience. One responsibility of teachers is to critically assess these assumptions and presuppositions in light of current conditions and socio-environmental trends. Through this process of identification and assessment of specific assumptions, beliefs, and values, the teacher is able to contribute to a process of cultural renewal.

Outmoded Assumptions, Beliefs, and Values

1. Progress involves the increased availability of consumer goods

   • "Their success allowed them to increase production."
   • "In many economies little is produced except what people need to stay alive.... If there are raw materials such as minerals, the people of the nation may have to ask others to come and show them how to develop their resources."

2. Progress involves greater ability to use technology to control and exploit the environment

   • "With these new techniques, farmers are no longer at the mercy of Mother Nature."
   • "Man is the only animal capable of changing his environment rather than adapting to it."

3. Science provides the best means of understanding and dealing with ecological problems

   • "Biological research continues to help us better understand environmental problems."

4. Viewing the environment as a resource for meeting human needs

   • "Our planet," "Our environment."
   • "There are two kinds of natural resources. One kind is said to be renewable. The other kind of natural resource is non-renewable. Once a non-renewable is used, it cannot be replaced."

5. The individual is viewed as autonomous and self-directing

   • "Having rights does not mean that we can do exactly as we please. One big responsibility, or duty, is to respect the rights of other people. It is up to each of us to make 'rights' work" (from elementary textbook discussion that presupposes rights, responsibilities, etc. to be a matter of individual choice).

6. Technological change is viewed as an expression of progress

   - "Advances in high technology have made the United States a leader among developed nations."
   - "Schools lack the computer hardware to make them truly efficient."

7. Experts are more likely to enable us to resolve problems because they do not rely upon traditional forms of knowledge

   - "The engineers provided the 'know-how' and the local community provided the muscle."
   - "Nutritional experts have become increasingly critical of what Americans eat."

8. Modern cultures have a more enlightened way of thinking than traditional ("primitive") cultures

   - "Advanced nations," "up-to-date views," "modern improvements," etc.
   - "We have long discarded older, less effective methods of farming."

9. Thinking of the environment in terms of component parts, and how to better manage these component parts, is progressive

   - "The trees in a forest are an example of a renewable resource. Only the full-grown trees are cut for logs. If new trees are planted and cared for, the forest will be renewed."

10. There is no limit to human progress

   - "With each generation of new computers, this technology becomes more and more powerful."
   - "People will always seek more information and better opportunities."

11. Responsibility is primarily to oneself or one's species

   - Discussions, presentations, etc. that reinforce a self-centered or anthropocentric understanding of relationships; i.e., "A community is a group of people," "Only you can decide what you value," or "All people have individual rights."

GUIDE #6:
MATHEMATICS LESSON

Teaching a mathematics lesson is a process of primary socialization and thus involves the close interaction of culture, language, and thought processes. As in other areas of the curriculum, success in teaching concepts is, in part, dependent upon being sensitive to metacommunication about classroom relationships.

A. Framing the Lesson

1. Makes the framing of critical aspects of the lesson explicit

   - The introduction involves a review of relevant concepts and the closure provides a summary as well as a sense of connectedness with the next lesson: "These exercises on graphing use what we have already learned about linear equations," "We'll come back next week to talk more about negative numbers."

2. Provides a good overview of key concepts

   - "Let's start today by looking at this chart, I'll explain it, you'll have a chance to ask questions, and we'll finish up by solving some problems on the board."

3. Good discussion of the connections that exist between sections of the book

   - "Logarithmic functions are related to exponential functions because…"

4. Key concepts are identified and explained as part of a discovery lesson

   - "All of these examples that we've looked at can be worked out using a number line."

5. Expectations are clearly established—and consistently reinforced

   - "You may have noticed that the text will always set the problems up for you to solve for Y."

B. Primary Socialization

1. Avoids misrepresenting axioms, numbers, and operations as facts

   - "In math we use the term *rational* (or *whole* or *real*) number in a technical, not literal sense."

2. Provided historical perspective that enabled students to understand the connection between theories of mathematics and social development

   - "This statistic was developed in the context of agricultural research"; "These types of equations became important to work in aeronautics when…."

3. Recognizes that metaphors used in mathematics may have different meanings for students

   • Consider: function, radical, revolution, relation, equals, etc.

4. Uses analogies and application problems that are familiar to students

   • "Let me talk about population growth as a way of introducing exponential functions"; "Taxes, the GNP, budgets, and food information labeling all use percentages"; "Instead of one quarter times one half, you may want to read this one quarter of one half."

C. Orchestrating the Social Ecology: Cultural and Gender Issues

1. Avoids reinforcing cultural orientation towards competitive individualism

   • Competitive individualism is often conveyed through games and grading practices where one student's gain is another student's loss: "The first one finished with this exercise I'll give extra points."
   • Teacher encourages students to work together: "If I'm busy, you can ask someone sitting nearby how they worked the problem"; "Today I'd like you to work with a partner on the chapter six exercises."

2. Creates a gender-fair classroom: Women and men represented equitably in pictures on the wall, organization of desks (including teacher's) fosters cooperation and ease of communication among all participants

   • Teacher notes the contributions of women as well as men to mathematics, including such individuals as Hypatia, Caroline Herschel, Sophie Germain, Mary Fairfax Somerville, Sonya Corvin-Krukovsky Kovalevsky, and Emmy Noether.

3. Avoids use of masculine oriented language, including the telling of sexist jokes and stories

   • Including "you guys," forms of locker room humor, overgeneralized use of masculine pronouns, and use of stereotyped examples (e.g., women depicted only in domestic settings).

4. Avoids leaving students with impression that mathematically based knowledge is culturally neutral

   • "This is more than just a matter of logic and following the rules." "Mathematicians don't just lock themselves up in some little room somewhere...."

GUIDE #7:
SCIENCE LESSON

Like other areas of the curriculum, the teaching of science involves implicit learning that may influence both the student's understanding of concepts and their attitude toward the role of science in society. Modeling, orchestrating social relationships, and being sensitive to culturally based misconceptions about the nature and limits of scientific knowledge are essential aspects of a positive classroom environment.

A. Creating an Atmosphere Conducive to Learning

1. Models safe behavior in carrying out experiments and using equipment
   - Wears goggles, apron, gloves, or other protection when appropriate.
   - Safe treatment of equipment (e.g., glass containers), chemicals, electricity, plants, and animals.
   - Disposes of chemicals in a safe and environmentally sound manner.

2. Models concern and value for living organisms in the classroom
   - Plants, animals, and equipment are well cared for.

3. Students are grouped so as to encourage a shared sense of responsibility
   - Use of lab partners and group projects.

4. Students are given responsibility for development and care of different aspects of the environment
   - Teacher encourages students to take responsibility for the care of lab materials, the cleaning and feeding of animals, care of plants, etc.

5. Achievements of women scientists are represented fairly
   - In books, pictures on walls, class discussions, illustrations, etc.

B. Teaching Style (teacher is available and responsive to all students)

1. Moves throughout the classroom lab
   - Checks on student understanding, clarifies purpose of the science lesson or activity, asks and responds to questions.

2. Facilitates interaction among students in a manner that brings recognition to the achievements of all students
   - Teacher's group and individual praise is genuine, without gender bias (see Guide #10) or neglect of students perceived as less able.
   - Offers context-specific assistance and recommendations: e.g., a middle school biology teacher tells a small lab group, "When you're finished with your work here, you might want to go over and see how the group at the back table took a different approach to this problem."

C. Avoiding Common Misconceptions (teacher helps students recognize the cultural and tentative nature of scientific knowledge)

1. Helps students understand the domains of social life where scientific knowledge has authority, and where it does not
   - E.g., resolving moral issues and questions of human value in such areas as social policy, government funding of research, and animal rights.

2. Recognizes that all observations are theory driven and thus may be partially subjective and culturally influenced
   - Theory-driven observations can be illustrated in areas of research ranging from plate tectonics to molecular biology.

3. Recognizes that scientific knowledge is tentative
   - "At this time, most scientists believe...."
   - The tentative nature of scientific knowledge is highlighted by examples of change in the recognized number of elements and in theories of evolution, the origins of the universe, the particulate nature of light, etc.

4. Uses vocabulary that is within the experience of students, and adds new terminology only as necessary to the introduction of new concepts
   - Examples of vocabulary that is sometimes introduced unnecessarily include words such as gradient, entropy, equilibrium, inflorescence, hirsute, tropism, and other largely technical descriptive terminology.

5. Avoids anthropomorphic descriptions of natural phenomena
   - "The electron wants to return to a lower energy level."

6. View of the planet is organismic rather than atomistic (root metaphor)
   - The organismic view emphasizes patterns of interaction and interdependency (plant as part of an ecology), while the atomistic view suggests self-containment.

7. Recognizes and discusses with students the manner in which technology may lead to exploitation of the social and natural environment
   - Including examples of pollution resulting from pesticides, nuclear testing, or other technological developments.

8. Recognizes that all measurement contains an element of error reflecting the physiological limitations of our senses and the selection-amplification characteristics of the measuring instruments
   - Including the use of microscopes, scales, clocks, etc.

9. Appreciates the uniqueness of each living form, and understands that classification is an arbitrary (culturally influenced) process created to simplify inquiry
   - e.g., the Linnaeus system: kingdom, phylum, class, order, etc.

10. Understands that science is influenced by the social, cultural, and political context in which it is carried out, and that scientific knowledge, in turn, alters that context—often in a permanent way
    - Consider issues related to SDI, cold fusion, substance abuse, birth control, telecommunications, etc.

11. Models and communicates a thoughtfulness about the cultural consequences of scientific inquiry and resulting technology; also helps clarify that it is never possible to anticipate all the consequences of scientific inquiry in advance
    - Discusses examples of unanticipated social consequence such as pollution, use of appropriate technology in other countries, or issues related to political equality.

GUIDE #8:
NONVERBAL PATTERNS OF COMMUNICATION

Metacommunication—that is, communication about what is being communicated—involves changes in body posture, voice pitch, use of longer or shorter pauses, change in gaze, laughter, spatial distance, and so forth. These are only part of the "vocabulary" of nonverbal communication used to establish a fuller sense of the context and nature of the interpersonal relationships within which verbal messages are shared and interpreted.

A. Proxemics (the classroom use of space)

1. Use of space appropriate to what is being communicated

   • Positioning: "private" messages conveyed in close proximity, public messages conveyed at greater distance; lectures given standing; discussion sitting down (at eye level).

2. Praises and responds to students regardless of where (front or back) they sit in the classroom

   • Calls on and maintains eye contact with students in back and side rows of the classroom.

3. Attends to relationship between spatial distance and level of student participation

   • Students seated in circle or semi-circle for discussion; students appropriate distance from one another for interacting.

4. Uses space as a signal or as a way of reframing the focus of classroom activities (teacher has established patterns whereby students recognize positioning as a cue)

   • Teacher stands at the front-center of classroom (or some other specific location) where she/he wants the students' attention; student desks arranged in variable ways for different activities; attention given to student comfort in demonstrating or illustrating a point.

B. Kinesics (body language)

1. Uses smile and head nodding to create positive classroom ambience

   • These gestures used to acknowledge a student's bid to speak, encourage student comments, written work, etc.

2. Appropriate eye contact with students

   • Amount and quality of eye contact that is appropriated depends on the students' dominant culture. Teachers responsive to these cultural dif-

ferences tailor their patterns of eye contact with different students in ways that avoid intimidation or an awkward reaction by the student. Look for varied patterns that increase "comfort level."
- Establishes eye contact without ignoring students who are perceived as low achievers.

3. Appropriate gaze during verbal exchanges with students
   - When a student is addressing a teacher, the teacher's gaze does not wander.

4. Body language is coordinated to communicate an attitude of caring and respect for students
   - Consider the following descriptions: In talking with students, the teacher would face them directly, lean or step in their direction, and maintain eye contact. At appropriate moments she would raise her eyebrows, nod her head, smile, and bring the index finger of her right hand up to her lips in a gesture of serious concentration. All of these nonverbal cues were coordinated to signal a coherent message: I care about what you have to say.

C. Prosody (voice patterns in the classroom)

1. Recognizes that longer pauses and slower tempo may be related to cultural differences and not intellectual ability
   - Teacher's tempo matches students—e.g., is attentive to "fast" talkers, patient with "slow" talkers, and will not stereotype students on this basis by viewing "slow" talkers as less academically able.
   - Teacher plans lessons in such a way as to give students adequate time for asking questions, contributing to class discussions, etc.

2. Extends "wait time" in order to encourage more student involvement
   - Pauses after questions, explanations, demonstrations, etc.

3. Tone, voice pitch, and rhythm communicate a sense of calmness and receptivity to student involvement
   - Teacher avoids "accusatory" tone of voice when asking students questions—"Why do you believe the moon goes around the earth?"

GUIDE #9:
ORCHESTRATION OF STUDENT INVOLVEMENT

The teacher exercises control over a number of social processes that are critically important to how students will perceive their rights and responsibilities in the classroom—and thus how they will participate in classroom activities. These include establishing the frame that influences how classroom activities are to be understood, allocating turns for participation in classroom discussions, and establishing whether the teacher-student relationship is based on the exercise of power or a sense of group solidarity.

A. Framing (establishing the boundaries and nature of relationships)

1. Teacher avoids the misunderstandings that result from some students not recognizing the frame within which the lesson is to be approached

   • Teacher names frame ("I want to tell you a story," "This is only one of many perspectives," "The purpose of this lesson...," etc.) or communicates frame indirectly by establishing patterns in nonverbal cues (see Guide #8), humor, or turn-taking.

2. When student questions or comments reframe what could be attended to in the lesson, teacher explores these new dimensions with the students

   • During a lecture on the river as a symbol in Mark Twain's *Huckleberry Finn*, a student asks a question about the historical context in which the novel was written, thus reframing the topic (from the novel itself to the historical setting) and the footing (from lecture to discussion). The teacher, in turn, acknowledges the student's question as a topic for discussion.

3. Frame is appropriate to the message and status relationship

   • Appropriate framing includes: nonverbal cues such as standing at the front of the room to help signal a "lecture" frame, sitting to signal discussion; lecture cues used with the whole class and not with individuals; or lecture used to "cover" material, discussion to explore ideas, seat work to practice skills, etc. Also, teacher balances use of humor, self-disclosure, personal comments, and so on with both role and instructional format.

4. Teacher names frame in order to re-establish control over direction of educational process

   • Includes such teacher comments as: "You must wait to read until after the class discussion," or "Let's take 15 minutes to review, then anyone who has a question will have a chance to ask it later."

B. Turn-Taking and Negotiation

1. Allocation of speaking turns is evenly distributed

    • Teacher provides opportunities and encourages all students (e.g., through "wait time," nonverbal cues, and specific praise) to participate in discussions/conversations.

2. Turn-taking rights are not limited to students who share the teacher's biases

    • A variety of students initiate speaking turns (or self-select), recognize others, self-evaluate their contributions, and share (limited) responsibilities for directing topic changes, pace, and level of participation.

3. Teacher negotiates with students over reasonable expectations for classroom behavior

    • Teacher accepts student use of humor, informal conversations, and differences of opinion when they do not undermine a conducive atmosphere for learning.

4. Teacher negotiates with students over reasonable expectations of intellectual performance (class assignments, participation in class discussions, and so forth)

    • Includes involving students directly in curricular decision making (e.g., by way of a class vote), providing options, using humor to promote solidarity, and flexible planning.

C. Power-Solidarity

1. Use of humor helps to establish a sense of solidarity between teacher and students

    • Teacher interprets students' humor as a bid for solidarity and shares that frame (the teacher, for example, is willing to laugh at him- or herself).

2. Teacher avoids inappropriate use of humor

    • Including using student as the object of a joke, humor that is perceived as ridiculing traditions and beliefs held by some students, sexist or racist jokes, and/or making others the object of scornful laughter.

3. Solidarity is appropriate to the professional judgments the teacher needs to make (evaluation, assignments, response to student behavior, and so forth), so that students do not feel betrayed in the relationship

    • Teacher does not pander, "play up to," or treat students as if they were peers (e.g., join students in ritual complaining or in criticizing an authority figure).

GUIDE #10:
GENDER AS A DIMENSION OF CLASSROOM RELATIONSHIPS

Gender bias may appear in many forms: the use of sexist language, humor that demeans and alienates, responding to student contributions in a differential manner that favors one gender group over another, and textbook examples that relate to masculine type experiences and foster masculine values and patterns of thinking.

A. Gender Bias in Language Use

1. Teacher avoids the use of masculine terms when referring to a mixed group of students

   • "You guys," "mankind," "he," etc., as in: "A company president should delegate his responsibilities with great care" and "A leader must be a man of persistence."

2. Balances emphasis on competitiveness and achievement with valuing the importance of caring relationships and cooperation

   • Teacher arranges classroom to facilitate cooperative, helping behavior between students. This might include setting up a tutoring system, small-group assignments, assigning students a "partner," or arranging desks in pairs, small groups, etc.

3. Provides examples in order to balance textbook illustrations, analogues, and stories that are derived from stereotyped masculine experience

   • Teacher is sensitive to masculine-oriented metaphors such as "the hard sciences," or from the field of computing, such metaphors as: "bomb," "command," "exploded file," "execute," "data capture," etc.

B. Unanticipated Consequences of Humor

1. Humor is not used to dismiss the class contributions of female students

   • An example of humor used to dismiss or belittle female contributions may take the form of an "isn't that cute" comment by the teacher followed by a quiet chuckle.

2. Teacher avoids use of teasing-type humor that causes discomfort and embarrassment for female students

   • Teasing or embarrassing humor includes jokes that make fun of a student's concern about looks, body, or (in adolescence) dating experiences.

3. Content of jokes is nonsexist

- Sexist jokes include those of the locker room genre or humor that may be prefaced with such comments as "only you guys will get this one."

C. Differential Treatment

1. Female students are called upon as often as male students

- In addition to simply counting responses, questions, and so on, here the supervisor may want to ask teachers whether they consciously use routines (such as calling on students systematically) to promote equity.

2. Uses same criteria in evaluating responses and providing assistance to both female and male students

- The teacher gives all students continuous guidance, and interprets, for example, achievement on the part of female students as attributed to effort rather than "talent."

3. Gender balance maintained in giving compliments and reinforcement (reward equity)

- Teacher compliments student ability, reinforces achievement, provides options, and makes opportunities or resources (e.g., books, "free" time, art materials, etc.) equally available to male and female students.

GUIDE #11:
CULTURALLY APPROPRIATE PARTICIPATION PATTERNS

The participation patterns that characterize learning processes in the student's primary culture should be taken into account when organizing the patterns of interaction that are to operate in the classroom. These patterns, which are generally taken for granted, are embedded in the assumptions and norms that constitute the culture's world view.

A. Avoiding Stereotyped Evaluations of Student Responses

1. Recognizes the ethnic and gender basis for differences in patterns of interaction and responses (i.e., does not treat all students as individuals who possess the same cultural package as the teacher)

   • Some students may have learned outside the school that it is wrong to compete with others at an individual level, answer questions or complete tasks where others have failed, make individual accomplishments public, accept direction from a single adult, maintain eye contact while speaking with an authority figure, publicly request information, etc.

2. Responds to student performance on the basis of cultural awareness as opposed to the stereotypes associated with a cultural group

   • Teacher monitors students and asks questions regarding the students' expectations and understandings of the school context (e.g., "What are your favorite activities in school, and why?" "What do you find difficult and what do you find easy?" "How would you explain this assignment to another student in the class?"

B. Participation Patterns—some may be culturally specific

1. Avoids spotlighting individual students during large-group instruction

   • Examples include directing questions, praise, etc. to groups of students rather than to individuals.

2. Encourages cooperative (vs. individualistic) behavior in the classroom (rewarding group effort and communication among students)

   • Examples include designing small-group activities that require a diversity of knowledge and skills, referring students to other students as a source of knowledge, offering group rewards, and arranging the physical space of the classroom to facilitate student-student interaction.

3. Does not assume that the teacher is the authority on what constitutes knowledge, and does not automatically strive to establish this authority

   - Sources of authority other than the teacher (e.g., traditions, folklore, community norms) are acknowledged through avoidance, at times, participation patterns where the teacher is at the center (metaphorically and literally) of classroom activities.

4. Gives equal authority to the spoken word as well as the written word

   - This includes developing a sensitivity to how the written word is often given a privileged status, as reflected in such comments as: "If you don't believe me, look in the textbook," "It wouldn't be in the book if it weren't important."

5. Neither takes for granted abstract, decontextualized, and linear patterns of thinking nor assumes the superiority of knowledge represented in the form of data and facts

   - Teacher avoids overreliance on abstract, decontextualized, and linear thought by using metaphors, narratives, and concrete examples in explaining an idea, concept, or skill (e.g., "shake hands with the racket," "the stock market crash was part of an economic downward spiral, like a giant whirlpool," or "one-half of one-fourth is one-eighth"—as opposed to "one-half times one-fourth equals one-eighth.")

6. Is sensitive to cultural differences in proxemic, kinesic, and prosodic patterns of communication

   - Depending on the cultural background of the student, a smile can signify rapport, embarrassment, or potential hostility; eye contact can signify respect or disrespect; close physical proximity can signify friendship or aggressiveness; and slow speech (relative to what the student takes as normal) can signify interest and consideration or rudeness and indifference.

7. Verbal interaction is maintained equally

   - Teacher asks questions, recognizes bids to speak, assigns seats, praises, and reprimands students in ways that do not disadvantage particular cultural groups.

About the Authors

C. A. BOWERS teaches education and social thought in the College of Education at the University of Oregon. His previous publications include *The Progressive Educator and the Depression: The Radical Years* (1969), *Cultural Literacy for Freedom* (1974), *The Promise of Theory: Education and the Politics of Cultural Change* (1984), *Elements of a Post-Liberal Theory of Education* (1987), *The Cultural Dimensions of Educational Computing: Understanding the Non-Neutrality of Technology* (1988) and (with David J. Flinders) *Responsive Teaching: An Ecological Approach to Classroom Patterns of Language, Culture, and Thought* (1990). His current interests concern the interconnections among education, belief systems, and the ecological crisis. He received his Ph.D. from the University of California, Berkeley.

DAVID J. FLINDERS is Assistant Professor of Education in the Department of Curriculum and Instruction at the University of Oregon. In addition to being coauthor (with C. A. Bowers) of *Responsive Teaching: An Ecological Approach to Classroom Patterns of Language, Culture, and Thought* (1990), he has published articles in *Curriculum Inquiry, The Journal of Curriculum and Supervision, and Educational Leadership,* and his dissertation won a notional award from the Association for Supervision and Curriculum Development. His interests concern curriculum foundations and qualitative classroom research. He received his doctoral degree from Stanford University in 1987.